SWAFFHAM to FAKENHAM

A Portrait in Old Picture Postcards

by

Gerald Lamont

S. B. Publications

First published in 1993 by S. B. Publications
c/o 19 Grove Road, Seaford, East Sussex, BN25 1TP

ISBN 1 85770 040 6

Typeset and printed by Geo. R. Reeve Ltd., Wymondham, Norfolk NR18 0BD.

CONTENTS

	page
The Picture Postcard	v
Introduction	vi

SWAFFHAM

	page
Novelty Pull-out Postcard	1
Camping Land and School	2
The Shire Hall	3
London Street	4
from the south	5
London Street	6
The Market Place	7
The Greyhound Hotel	8
The Market Cross	9
The Market Place	10
Empire Day	11
Cycling Club	12
Roman Catholic Church	13
Church of St. Peter and St. Paul	14
An Old Well	15
The Fountain	16
The Pedlar	17

	page
The Grammar School	18
A Hospital Sunday Parade	19
Lynn Street	20
'A' Squadron, Sherwood Rangers	21
The Market Place	22
Thomas Johnson, Gunmaker's Shop	23
The Central Cafe	24
The War Memorial	25
The Market Place	26
Mangate Street	27
Manor House Corner	28
Camp Life, 1912	29
The George Hotel	30
Station Road	31
Station Street	32
Castle Acre	33—37
Litcham	38—39
Tittleshall Church	40
Weasenham St. Peter	41—42
Raynham	43—44
Hempton	45—54

CONTENTS

FAKENHAM

	page		page
Gogg's Mill	55	The War Memorial	79—80
Comic Card	56	A Meet of Harriers	81
Aerial View	57	Fife and Forfar Yeomanry	82
Wells Road	58	Bridge Street	83
St. Anthony's Church	59	Norwich Street	84—87
The Grammar School	60	The Post Office	88
Wells Road	61—62	Aftermath of the Queen's Road Fire	89
Oak Street	63	Station Road	90
The Corn Exchange	64	Baron's Hall	91
The Post Office	65	Printing Works Fire	92
The Flood	66	The Cattle Market	93
Hall Staithe	67—68	Jubilee Bridge	94
Tunn Street	69	Fakenham Mill	95—96
Church of St. Peter and St. Paul	70	The Causeway	97—99
The Market Square	71	West Railway Station	100
The Crown Inn	72	Egg Depot	101
The Market Place	73	Bay House, Sculthorpe	102
Market Day	74—75	The Street, Sculthorpe	103
The Proclamation of George V	76	Grey's Mill, Sculthorpe	104
Norfolk Yeomanry on Parade	77	Bibliography & Acknowledgements	105
Peace Celebrations	78	S. B. Publications	106

Cover Picture: Raynham Hall, Fakenham.

THE PICTURE POSTCARD

The first postcard was posted, 1 October 1869, in Austria and was followed one year later by the first postcards in Britain. These were plain stationery cards with a halfpenny stamp printed on each card.

In 1894 there appeared the first of those picture postcards known as 'court cards'. These were smaller in size than today's cards, with at least one picture on one side and spaces for an address, a message and an adhesive stamp on the other. In time larger cards were used. These were allowed in Britain after 1 November, 1889.

From 1 January, 1902, a 'divided back' postcard, with a vertical line at the centre, was permitted. The front was characterised by·a full-sized picture or photograph.

This, the golden age of the postcard, continued until World War I, 1914 to 1918. It became traditional for each family to keep in a postcard album those cards sent by relations and friends.

Much of the topography of Edwardian Britain was uniquely captured in those fine postcards produced by the national publishers of the day. Several of these firms, such as Valentine's, Wrench and Frith's, sent their own photographs or commissioned locals to record street or river scenes, churches, monuments and scenic views in cities, towns or villages across the United Kingdom. These were in turn sold in picture postcard form in large numbers in local shops.

Those local photographers and publishers − who by their joint efforts were on hand to record fires, floods, parades and other neighbourhood events − were able to preserve for the historian, the postcard collector and for members of their own community an invaluable visual record of the past.

All the picture postcards used in this book are from the author's own collection.

INTRODUCTION

The postcards depicted follow a route from Swaffham to Fakenham:

We begin our journey on the southern side of Swaffham as it appeared in the first decade of this century. Like many other Norfolk market towns it had become dependent since Saxon times upon local agriculture; Swaffham's name is derived from the early Germanic tribes which settled in the region.

Its large Market Place, once the site of a butter market, is dominated by the Market Cross. The parish church of St. Peter and St. Paul, dating from the fifteenth century, is just to the east of this historic centre of commerce. John Chapman, the famous Swaffham Pedlar, is commemorated on carved effiges inside the church and also on a prominent town signpost. He is credited with the building of the north aisle in the church as a result of his fortuitous wealth. The town has had its share of less fortunate times, as in 1775, when a calamitous fire destroyed more than twenty houses in London Street.

Leaving Swaffham and continuing northwards we take the road to Fakenham. On our way we visit the historic village of Castle Acre, with its castle and ruined priory.

This is also a route to the coast and has been used by many visitors to Norfolk. We then pass both Weasenham St. Peter and East Raynham, after a detour to Litcham and Tittleshall, before reaching Hempton, Fakenham and Sculthorpe.

Fakenham, situated on gentle slopes that run down to the River Wensum, is particularly interesting, being mentioned in the Domesday Book as a royal manor of King Harold.

In 1373 the title of Lordship was granted to John of Gaunt, Duke of Lancaster, by his father, King Edward III, and the manor then became entitled Fakenham Lancaster. It remained a royal manor until the seventeenth century, when it was sold into private ownership.

The town is dominated by the parish church of St. Peter and St. Paul, with its fifteenth-century tower, a landmark which is visible for miles around. The Market Place and its adjoining square contain some fine buildings including those houses with their black-glazed tiles of local origin.

I hope the reader will gain as much pleasure from this book as I have in collecting the picture postcards and then compiling the captions for them. I hope it may revive memories of times past for those who have lived in Norfolk. Most of these postcards, to my knowledge, have never been published in book form before.

Gerald Lamont
Fakenham

NOVELTY PULL-OUT POSTCARD, c.1914

This novelty 'pull-out' postcard published by Valentine's, has twelve views of Swaffham and district and is folded in concertina fashion behind the soldier's cap. The sender is a soldier who seeks a 'pass' home. He knows of someone who has obtained leave by saying that his wife is ill. The writer asks the recipient of the card to send 'news' of a family illness so that he similarly can use this as an excuse for leaving camp.

We Terriers get some Strange Views into our Heads at SWAFFHAM

CAMPING LAND AND SCHOOL, SWAFFHAM, c.1908

This piece of land was bequeathed to the parishioners of Swaffham in 1463, by the Reverend John Botewright. It was to be used for archery, games, military drill and for the ancient game of 'kicking camp', an early form of football. Sited on the Camping Land and built in 1838 is the National Boys' School. The original Hamond's School, founded by Nicholas Hamond in 1724, stood on the left of the picture.

S 2785   SHIRE HALL, SWAFFHAM.

THE SHIRE HALL, SWAFFHAM, p.u. 1910

Designed by John Brown of Norwich, the Norfolk County Surveyor, the Shire Hall was built in 1839 and became the seat of the Norfolk County Justices. The former Swaffham Prison, which closed in 1880, is to be seen at the rear of the building. To the right is a weights and measures office once used by the former inspector, W.J. Barry.

LONDON STREET, SWAFFHAM, c.1906

This view of London Street looks south and away from the town centre. The former Black Horse public house and Preston's butcher's shop, with the butcher outside, are on the left. Another former inn, the Spread Eagle, stands on the right. Today, the ornate ironwork which supported the inn's sign is still visible. The traffic on the road consists of a horse-drawn milkcart and a knife-grinder pushing his handcart.

SWAFFHAM FROM THE SOUTH, c.1949

Swaffham on a busy Saturday market day in the late 1940s. The town was granted the right to a market in the early part of the thirteenth century and became the market centre for a large surrounding area. Also shown are market stalls for furniture and local produce. A livestock auction is in progress in the distance, on the right, outside the Greyhound Hotel.

LONDON STREET, SWAFFHAM, c.1910

London Street as it appeared looking south from the Market Place towards The Town Pit. Pit Lane is to the left and is fronted by the family butcher's shop of D.L. Bloom. This later became an antique and secondhand furniture shop. The building with the imposing front, formerly the Wesleyan Chapel, is now Swaffham's Methodist Chapel.

MARKET PLACE, SWAFFHAM. J 6915.

THE MARKET PLACE, SWAFFHAM, p.u.1927

A near deserted Market Place with only a horse-drawn cart and a bull-nosed Morris motor car. In the background the Greyhound Hotel offers Steward and Patteson's ales and stout, delivered from the local Swaffham brewery in Cley Road. The Town Pit, on the right, has now been filled in.

THE GREYHOUND HOTEL, SWAFFHAM, c.1910

A young boy and two soldiers are seen outside Swaffham's Greyhound Hotel, which is situated on the eastern side of the Market Place. Built in 1776 and named after the Earl of Orford, the hotel commemorated the founding in the same year of England's first coursing club, at Swaffham. Prior to the Greyhound, a public house named the Bluebell stood on this site. Every Saturday, furniture auctions are still held in front of the hotel, whilst to the rear, vegetables, poultry and rabbits are sold.

THE MARKET CROSS, SWAFFHAM, c.1927

The classical Market Cross consists of eight stone pillars capped by a dome surmounted by the Roman Goddess of corn, Ceres, which stands on the southern edge of Swaffham Market Place. The Cross was given to the town in 1783 by the Earl of Orford, who took residence in the town during the coursing season.

Market ·Place, Swaffham

Valentines Series

THE MARKET PLACE, SWAFFHAM, c.1910

The Market Place looking towards Lynn Road. On the right are the Assembly Rooms built in 1817 for Hunt Balls and other notable social occasions. In their original state these rooms were lavishly decorated with ceiling chandeliers and many wall oil paintings. In contrast troops were billeted there during the Second World War.

EMPIRE DAY, SWAFFHAM, 24 May, 1906

Empire Day celebrations at the Market Place Cross. Beyond the gathering, in the background, is the Red Lion public house.

SWAFFHAM CYCLING CLUB, 1 June, 1905
Members of Swaffham Cycling Club captured by Swaffham photographer, S.W. Hannant, on an outing to Oxborough.
Notice the tricycle..

ROMAN CATHOLIC CHURCH. SWAFFHAM. 56.

THE ROMAN CATHOLIC CHURCH, SWAFFHAM, c.1911

Swaffham's former Roman Catholic Church, dedicated to Our Lady of Pity, stands on the left of Theatre Street. This building was formerly a theatre and a builder's store before it became a place of worship, in 1911. When a more modern catholic church was built in Station Street, the earlier church was taken for use as a garage. In 1928 it was destroyed by fire.

S. S. Peter & Paul, Swaffham.

ST. PETER AND ST. PAUL, SWAFFHAM, c.1908

The building of this church began in 1454, under the rector, the Reverend John Botewright, Chaplain to Henry VI. It was completed with its west tower in 1510. This Barnack stone tower, housing eight bells, was capped by a needle spire. In its early days many valuable and rare books — including the Black Book of Swaffham with its story of John Chapman, the Swaffham Pedlar — were kept in an upper room of the church. Within the south transept is a monument to Catherine Stewart, the grandmother of Oliver Cromwell.

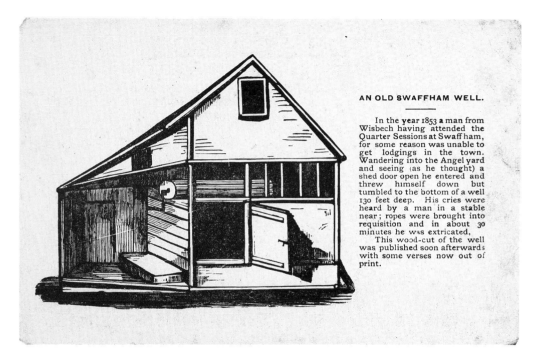

AN OLD SWAFFHAM WELL.

In the year 1853 a man from Wisbech having attended the Quarter Sessions at Swaffham, for some reason was unable to get lodgings in the town. Wandering into the Angel yard and seeing (as he thought) a shed door open he entered and threw himself down but tumbled to the bottom of a well 130 feet deep. His cries were heard by a man in a stable near; ropes were brought into requisition and in about 30 minutes he was extricated.

This wood-cut of the well was published soon afterwards with some verses now out of print.

AN OLD SWAFFHAM WELL, p.u.1915

A wartime card sent with New Year's greetings in 1915. The dramatic story described on the postcard occurred at one of thirty similar wells believed to have been located in Swaffham. Whilst some were in prominent street positions, others were less well-known, in public house yards or on private property.

15

THE FOUNTAIN, SWAFFHAM.

THE FOUNTAIN, SWAFFHAM, c.1910

The Bagge Memorial Fountain, erected in 1882 through public subscriptions, stood on the north-western side of the Market Place. The Memorial Fountain, which featured a bust of Sir William Bagge MP, and a drinking fount, was demolished in 1940. It is conceivable that the bellringer in the above photograph was summoning the children to school.

THE PEDLAR OF SWAFFHAM

The Swaffham town sign as shown was erected in the Market Place in 1912. The original wooden sign commemorated the story of John Chapman, the famous pedlar, and his dog. The popular story told is that Chapman, a Swaffham merchant, had a dream that if he went to London he would discover a treasure on London Bridge. He walked with his dog to the capital and met a man on the bridge who informed Chapman he also had a dream of a treasure hidden under a tree in the garden of 'a John Chapman of Swaffham, in Norfolk'. Returning home, the pedlar dug under a tree and found a hoard of treasure. With his new wealth, John financed the north aisle of Swaffham Church. Pew carvings still depict the pedlar, his wife and his dog. The present Swaffham town sign, which replaced the original, was erected in 1925.

THE GRAMMAR SCHOOL, SWAFFHAM, c.1906

Founded in 1724 by Nicholas Hamond, a member of a prominent Swaffham family, the original Hamond's Grammar School was built on The Camping Land, Swaffham. From there it was moved to the site shown above. Under reorganisation, in 1977, it was amalgamated with the Secondary Modern School to become Hamond's High, Comprehensive School, in Brandon Road. The building shown in the photograph has once again become a private residence.

Hospital Sunday, Swaffham.

A HOSPITAL SUNDAY PARADE, SWAFFHAM, p.u.1922

To raise funds for the building and for the maintenance of hospitals, before the advent of National Health Service, many communities held parades and carnivals. This photograph shows a parade entering Swaffham from Lynn Street. The shops of Howard, the saddler, and R.B. Yeomans, the boot-maker, are on the right. After the parade, the band went to the Market Place to play once more.

19

LYNN STREET, SWAFFHAM, c.1904

In the background beyond the town centre, the Waterworks, which opened 16 September, 1867, is marked by its tower. On the right is the former Primitive Methodist Chapel, which was later used, before demolition, by the Salvation Army. It is now the site of the Combined Services' Club.

'A' SQUADRON, SHERWOOD RANGERS, QUADLING'S FARM, SWAFFHAM, c.1912

The squadron is photographed at Quadling's Farm, Swaffham, by W. Cole Plowright. As a local specialist in army camp photography prior to the First World War, he conceivably visited other nearby camps at Manor Farm, Sporle Road and The Antinghams. William Quandling farmed at the above site, which stood at the corner of The West Acre Road and Spinner's Lane. This is now occupied by Swaffham Police Station.

THE MARKET PLACE, c.1933

The northern side of Swaffham Market Place shows C.V. Young's boot and shoe shop, with the proprietor and his staff standing outside. To the right is F. Sheldrick, baker and confectioner, advertising Hovis bread. Beyond, stood the former Prince of Wales Inn, which offered locally-brewed Steward and Patteson's beer. Their Swaffham brewery was in Cley Road, with their main works in Norwich, before they were taken over by Watneys.

THOMAS JOHNSON, GUNMAKER'S SHOP, SWAFFHAM, c.1920

Johnson's gunmaker's shop stands to the right of Ash Close in Swaffham. It is presumed that Mrs. Johnson, the owner's wife, is at the entrance to the shop. To her right is an interesting display of guns. Later, the shop's name was changed to Thomas Johnson and Sons. Today it is occupied by an estate agent.

THE CENTRAL CAFE, SWAFFHAM, c.1935

A fine example of a shopfront of the period. Mr. C. Hawkins, the proprietor, stands at the doorway entrance. To his right is a variety of goods which included an unusual assortment of woollen and tobacco merchandise. Several cigarette vending machines are fixed to the wall on the left. A set of personal weighing scales is also visible. A cafe and restaurant complete the facilities in this building, which is to the left of Ash Close, leading to Spinners Lane. Formerly the Prince of Wales public house, this 1930s shop is now a laundrette.

WAR MEMORIAL, SWAFFHAM.

H.6918.

THE WAR MEMORIAL, SWAFFHAM, c.1950

The war memorial, which honours those servicemen who gave their lives for their country during the two world wars, is situated in the north-eastern corner of the Market Place. This was a popular position for parking vehicles in the 1950s, as the number of Austin Seven motor cars shown would indicate. One bears the registration HV 4963. Later, protective iron railings were erected around the memorial.

Market Place — Swaffham

Gibson & Co., Gateshead

THE MARKET PLACE, SWAFFHAM, c.1904

Horse sales were conducted behind the railings on the left. The building in the centre was built, in 1858, as the Corn Hall.
It included a library, a reading room and a Young Men's Institute, with a billiard room. When the card was published, the
building was in use as the Salvation Army Citadel. Today it is the local Job Centre.

MANGATE STREET, SWAFFHAM, c.1911

Mangate Street was formerly known as Block Street. The ivy-covered house on the left served as a flour merchant's and a baker's shop and advertised 'Darren Bread Best For Health' on its enamel signs. The house in the left foreground was demolished to facilitate a rear entrance to the George Hotel. On the right is the churchyard.

MANOR HOUSE CORNER, SWAFFHAM, c.1911

This road leads into Swaffham from East Dereham. The route to the right, leads to Sporle. Further on, behind Swaffham's magnificent cedar tree, stands Manor Farm House. A field adjacent to the farm was used, before the First World War, as an army camp and became flooded during the heavy storms in August 1912. In the foreground an ornate lamp-post overlooks the old timber signpost.

CAMP LIFE AT SWAFFHAM, p.u.1912

These bell tents stand flooded on the Sporle Road Army Camp site. Torrential storms, 6 August, 1912, caused similar widespread havoc across the county of Norfolk. The Second Battalion of the Grenadier Guards, camping here at the time, were transferred to the Assembly Rooms in Swaffham for the duration of the storms.

SWAFFHAM 1912 26

THE GEORGE HOTEL, SWAFFHAM, c.1912

The George Hotel stands on the eastern side of the junction of the Fakenham, Dereham, and King's Lynn Roads. This postcard shows officers who have stayed at the hotel, having also stabled their horses there, preparing to move off. The George's amenities included a bowling green and a billiard room. The top floor windows, with ornate shell decoration surrounds, replaced the earlier dormer ones when the hotel was renovated in 1909. The printing works of local postcard publisher, J.A. Gould, stood opposite to the George. Out of view, on the left, next to the hotel, stood a confectionery shop/tea room owned by Fred Lane.

Swaffham   Station Road

The Wrench Series No. 9694

STATION ROAD, SWAFFHAM, c.1905

Station Road, sometimes known as Castle Acre Road, leaves Swaffham and heads north towards Fakenham. The office of G.E. Kenny and Co., corn-cake and coal merchants, is on the left. Their depots were in Swaffham Station Yard, Fakenham and Upwell. Further down on the left of Station Road is the White Lion Inn, now closed. J. F. Impson's Building Yard is on the right.

Station Street, Swaffham. 112276.

STATION STREET, SWAFFHAM, c.1927

On the left, at the corner of Station Street and Spinners Lane, is Pye and Wilson, poulterer's and family butcher's shop. They also had another shop in London Street. To the right of the butcher's corner shop are the premises of A.G. Wright, motor engineer. Later, Oliver Meek, basket-maker, moved into them from the opposite side of Station Street. The twin towers of Swaffham Baptist Chapel, erected in 1922, rise above the other buildings. In the distance are the level-crossing gates near Swaffham Railway Station. On the right, in Station Street, stands Swaffham's cinema. Originally known as the Electric Picture Drome, it was built just after the First World War by Mr. Gay Brearley. Still later, it became known as the Regal, but closed in 1964, and is now used as a factory.

CASTLE ACRE, c.1930

Five views of Castle Acre. Top left is the Priory, whilst top right shows the Gateway to Bailey Street. In the latter scene the Central Stores of W. Peacock is to the left of the Gateway. The ford across the River Nar is shown at bottom left, and bottom right shows Stocks Green in the heart of the village. In the centre of the postcard is the fifteenth-century church, which was dedicated to St. James.

Stocks Green looking East, Castleacre

STOCKS GREEN, CASTLE ACRE, p.u.1924

The sender of this postcard drew an 'x' on the picture to mark the post office where she posted the card. Miss Elizabeth Nicholds was the sub-postmistress there at the time.

CASTLE ACRE WAR MEMORIAL, c.1920
A large assembly gathers for the dedication service and the unveiling of Castle Acre's War Memorial. It occupies a prominent site on Stocks Green at the village centre. In the right background is the Ostrich Inn.

St. James Church, Castleacre

ST. JAMES' CHURCH, CASTLE ACRE, c.1920

Built principally in the perpendicular style, the fifteenth-century parish church of St. James stands on an elevated site in the valley of the River Nar. With a chancel, a nave, a north and south aisle, it is a fine example of a Norfolk parish church. Its embattled western tower features a porch on its northern side. St. James' is also notable for its use of quoins, flint and dressed stone buttresses. Restoration work was undertaken in 1846 and 1875.

THE PRIORY, CASTLE ACRE

These ruins in the valley of the River Nar were photographed by H. Cave of East Dereham, who had a shop in Swaffham. Castle Acre Priory was originally administered by the monastic order of the Cluniacs. This branch of the Benedictines, reformed by Bernard De Clugni in A.D. 912, was responsible for a total of thirty-five religious houses in England. William de Warrenne's Great Priory at Lewes was the principal Cluniac house. Castle Acre Priory is now maintained by the Department of the Environment.

THE BRIDGE, LITCHAM.

THE BRIDGE, LITCHAM, p.u.1903

Church Street winds out of the village of Litcham and over the old brick bridge that spanned the River Nar. The bridge has now been replaced by a more modern structure, and the road has been widened. Priory House, on the left, was once a resting place for pilgrims.

LITCHAM, c.1935

The King's Arms, Litcham, advertises Steward and Patteson's Ales on its sign in the left foreground. To the right, behind the houses, is the Parish Church of All Saints. This has a red brick tower built by Matthew Halcot, prior to his death in 1675. A central interior pillar of the church bears a prayer, signed by Wyke Bamburg, believed to be a pilgrim making his way to the shrine at Walsingham.

4853 TITTLESHALL CHURCH,

ST. MARY'S CHURCH, TITTLESHALL

The ancient church at Tittleshall is dedicated to St. Mary. Principally built of stone, in the Gothic style, its features include a chancel, a nave, a south porch and an embattled western tower with clock. Inside the church is a monument to Holkham's Sir Thomas Coke KB, and members of his family.

THE GREEN, WEASENHAM ST. PETER, c.1920

Weasenham St. Peter, with its open village green and ponds, remains largely unspoilt to this day. The post office on the extreme right served both Weasenham St. Peter and the nearby village of Weasenham All Saints. Sadly, both the post office and the adjacent village stores have now been closed.

THE VICARAGE, WEASENHAM ST. PETER, c.1920

An idyllic rural scene at the vicarage of Weasenham St. Peter. The vicar's famly and their housemaids gather at the porch entrance for this photograph. Note the child's toy horse to the right of the picture. This vicarage was eventually annexed with that of the adjoining village of Weasenham All Saints.

H. J. HEYHOE, CHEMIST.   RAYNHAM HALL   FAKENHAM.

RAYNHAM HALL, p.u.1904

Raynham Hall, a redbrick house with a stone dressing, was built in the early seventeenth-century for Sir Roger Townshend. His design was influenced by Inigo Jones. The master mason, William Edge, is buried at Saint Martin's Church, South Raynham. It is reported that when Captain Frederick Marryat, the sailor and novelist, stayed at the hall, he saw the ghost of The Brown Lady. When he discharged his pistol at the apparition, the bullet passed through the spectre and lodged in a door.

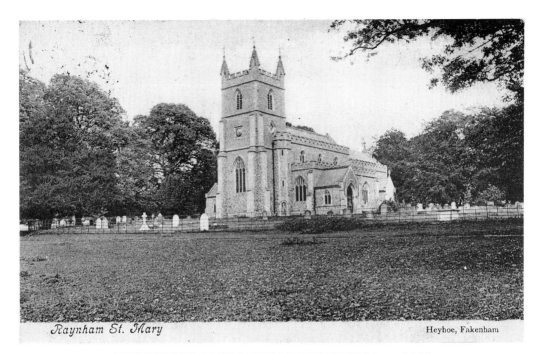

Raynham St. Mary

Heyhoe, Fakenham

THE CHURCH OF ST. MARY, EAST RAYNHAM, p.u.1906

The church stands in the picturesque setting of Raynham Park. Rebuilt in 1868, in the perpendicular style, the church architects were Clark and Holland. In the north aisle is a brass effigy of Sir Robert Godfrey, who died in 1522. He is portrayed in his academic robes. Further features are the church's marquetry panels and a chest, dated 1602, near the doorway entrance.

ON THE RAYNHAM ROAD

RAYNHAM ROAD, HEMPTON, c.1904

Just outside Fakenham is Hempton's Raynham Road. The route shown to the left leads to Swaffham. Out of view to the right, stood the Bullseye Cottages, so named because of a prominent and round central window. Whilst these cottages have now been demolished, the one to the left remains.

HEMPTON GREEN, Norfolk.

HEMPTON GREEN, p.u.1904

Sheep graze on the large expanse of common land known as Hempton Green. This overlooks the town of Fakenham. In the central background the tall chimney marks the site of Hempton's brickworks and kilns in Shereford Road. The Green was also the location of Fakenham's nine-hole golf course, one of the earliest in Norfolk. On other occasions, Hempton Green has been used for football and cricket matches, and as a grassed airstrip.

HEMPTON GREEN, p.u.1905

This view of Hempton Green shows Hempton Windmill towering above the cottages on the Shereford Road. The Old Buck Inn to the right, formerly known as 'The Sign of the Deer's Head', had its own brewery to the rear of the premises. Later, before being demolished to make way for Fakenham's western bypass, it became a private residence.

Hempton Mill and Common, Fakenham.   93243.

HEMPTON MILL AND COMMON, FAKENHAM, c.1922

This 1920s view of Hempton Windmill shows the mill without its sails. It was demolished in 1944 because it lay in a direct line between the Fakenham Church tower and the West Raynham R.A.F. airfield. German bomb-bearing aircraft made use of it in wartime as a landmark until it was removed. The mill rubble was then laid to help prepare the runways at nearby Sculthorpe Airfield. Though Mill House, to the left, still remains, some of the other buildings have been demolished recently.

BUTTERFLY ROW, HEMPTON, c.1905

The tower of Fakenham Parish Church is just visible above the rooftops of Butterfly Row, Hempton. The larger, end-of-terrace houses were built with the coming of the railways to Hempton. The scene is little changed today.

HEMPTON GREEN, c.1905

The brick and flint cottages of Front Street look out today over Hempton Green, very much as they did in 1905 in this postcard. The former King's Head, seen in the right background, is now a school of dance. The village pump, in the foreground, is still standing, however the railings have been removed. The pump is no longer in working order..

Hempton Green Fair.　　　　　　　　BRITANNIA SERIES.　No. 790

HEMPTON GREEN FAIR, c.1905

Children are seen enjoying the swing boats which were part of the activities organised to coincide with the sheep fairs held on Hempton Green every September. The Hempton Green fairs replaced earlier ones at Harpley and Kipton. The first of these took place on 2 September, 1848, and the final one on 3 September, 1969, which was the last sheep fair in Norfolk.

AFTER THE STORM

May Bone, a local photographer, published this remarkable postcard showing adults, children and dogs grouped on the Hempton side of the River Wensum, around this large uprooted tree. Bone had a photographer's studio in Fakenham and also sold postcards from the kiosk at the entrance to Hunstanton Pier.

River Wensum, Fakenham.

THE RIVER WENSUM, p.u.1905

Wensum is believed to be a translation from Old English and means 'winding'. On this postcard, published by Stewartson's of Fakenham, a sailing boat glides gently downstream towards the back of Gogg's Mill, Hempton. The rear view of the mill was less attractive than that of the front and few postcards were published showing this aspect of it. A road traffic bridge forming part of Fakenham's western bypass now occupies this site.

HEMPTON MILL.

HEMPTON MILL, c.1908

Gogg's Mill, Hempton from the Hempton side of the River Wensum. This view was much favoured by artists and photographers, and a large number of picture postcards was published showing the mill and its adjoining residence. Named after Thomas Gogg, the mill owner, the main structure of the building was demolished in 1934. However, parts of the walls, other brickwork and the bridge still survived until 1952.

Gogg's Mill,
Fakenham.

GOGG'S MILL AND FAKENHAM LANCASTER CREST, p.u.1906

The watermill, with the miller's residence, the footbridge and the ford to the right of the main building, shown on the Fakenham side of the River Wensum. This postcard was published by Stoddard and Company of Halifax, as one of their Ja-Ja series of heraldic cities and towns. The river appears to be much wider than it is today.

If you've got the hump come to FAKENHAM.

COMIC CARD, FAKENHAM

This comic card was designed by the well-known artist, Reg Carter. Reginald Arthur Lee Carter, 1856—1950, was born and lived for most of his life in Southwold, Suffolk. A member of the North British Academy, he contributed to *The Sketch*, *The Tatler* and other similar magazines. As a versatile and prolific artist of postcards, he worked for a number of publishers including himself. This card would have been printed and overlaid with the names of many different cities, towns and villages.

AERIAL VIEW OF FAKENHAM

AEROFILMS SERIES   AERIAL VIEW OF FAKENHAM   21282

AERIAL VIEW OF FAKENHAM

This aerial view of Fakenham on market day was published by Aerofilms of Hendon, who also advertised that enlargements were available. In the foreround, to the left, is the parish church of St. Peter and St. Paul. Next to this is the Corn Hall. What is now the Queen's Road car park is seen as a tennis court in this photograph.

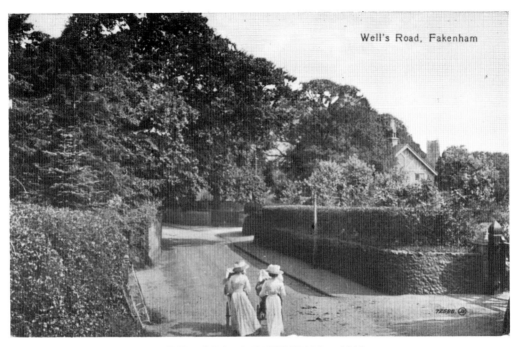

Well's Road, Fakenham

WELLS ROAD, FAKENHAM, c.1910

A view from an early Valentine's series of postcards. To the left of Wells Road is Field Lane. The entrance to the Roman Catholic Church of St. Anthony of Padua is to the right. The quiet rural aspect of Wells Road, apparently being enjoyed by the ladies with their prams, has long since disappeared.

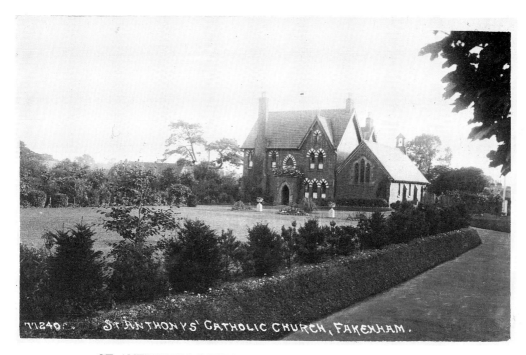

ST. ANTHONY'S CATHOLIC CHURCH, FAKENHAM, c.1911

The Roman Catholic Church of St. Anthony of Padua overlooks its own spacious gardens. Catholics are believed to have used various locations in Fakenham to celebrate mass before the beginning of the twentieth century. In 1905, the Reverend H. Gray used his own home, 'Wensum House', in Hempton, as a catholic centre of worship. Between 1908 and 1911 the present church was built on a site adjacent to Wells Road. The message on this card reads, 'I hope you think this is a pretty picture. Fakenham itself is a dear little place. There is a "Quality Street" look about the houses.'

6071 GRAMMAR SCHOOL, FAKENHAM

THE GRAMMAR SCHOOL, FAKENHAM, c.1952

The attractive building shown was originally known as Highfield House and was built by the Campbell family in 1820. Standing in its own large grounds, and later passing into the possession of the Digby family, it was bought in 1922 for use as a secondary modern school. An extension to the right of the main structure was opened in 1930 by Lord Leicester. It was eventually acquired for use as a grammar school and further additions were made.

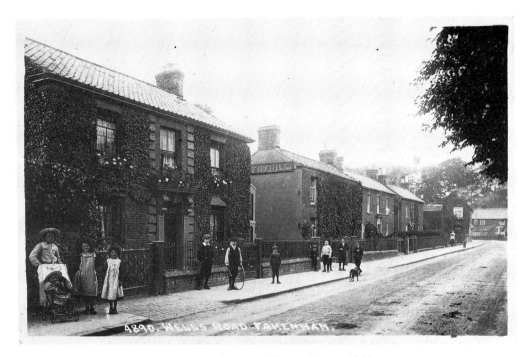

WELLS ROAD, FAKENHAM, p.u.1918

A charming scene in Wells Road, Fakenham. Several groups of children gather for the photographer. Whilst each child wears a hat, one young boy has his whip and hoop to hand. All the houses, with the exception of those known as The Pound Cottages, at the top of the road, remain standing today. Behind the second house on the left was Miss B.A. Tuthill's millinery warehouse, with its ladies' blouses, hosiery, lingerie and general underwear.

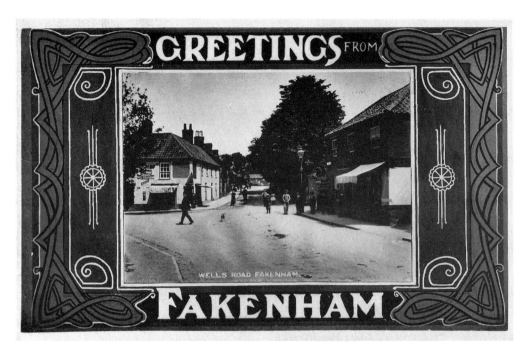

GREETINGS FROM FAKENHAM

WELLS ROAD FAKENHAM.

WELLS ROAD, FAKENHAM, p.u.1906

This is the view looking from Oak Street into Wells Road. To the left is Nelson Road, with G. Tuck's baker's shop clearly in view. This later became an antique shop, then a second-hand bookshop which has now closed. The wall postbox in the former baker's shop still remains today. To the right from Wells Road is Constitution Hill.

OAK STREET, FAKENHAM, p.u.1914

This postcard was sent to a British soldier serving in France in 1914, to remind him of home. The house on the left, known as 'The Oaks' was built in 1766 and was demolished in 1967. The King Edward VII Coronation Memorial is now located here. Raised through public subscription in 1902, the Memorial stood in the Market Place and then later was moved to the northern side of the Corn Hall. The Royal Oak public house stood to the left, further down Oak Street, and was adjacent to the Wesleyan Chapel. This became the Salvation Army Citadel and was destroyed by a bomb in the Second World War. It was the only Fakenham building to be severely damaged in this way and was rebuilt in 1967.

Corn Exchange, Fakenham.

THE CORN EXCHANGE, FAKENHAM

This postcard, with its 'undivided back' suggesting it was published before 1902, uses a very early picture of the Corn Exchange. This was built in 1855 at a cost of £4,000. The Exchange, together with the Assembly Rooms as shown above, was covered with a large glass dome. John Brown of Norwich, the Norfolk County Surveyor and designer of this building, was also responsible for a series of others. These included the workhouses at Lingwood, Great Yarmouth and Docking, a yarn mill in Norwich, a church at Hainford and the Shire Hall at Swaffham. The Corn Exchange was used as a reading room, a library and as a magistrates' court until, in 1934, it became the Central Cinema. This closed in 1976 and is now the Central Bingo Club.

THE POST OFFICE, FAKENHAM, c.1908

Just around the corner from Hall Staithe, in Old Post Office Street, stood Fakenham's first crown post office. This replaced an earlier sub-post office in this street. When it was closed down here, it was moved to the eastern side of the Market Place and then, in 1933, to its present site at the junction of Holt Road and Queen's Road.

THE FLOOD, FAKENHAM, August 1912

This scene, photographed from the Corn Hall rooftop, is that looking out across Old Post Office Street and over the flooded meadows towards Hempton. Here the line of the River Wensum is just visible. In the bottom right-hand corner a crowd of onlookers stands at the water's edge, in Hall Staithe.

HALL STAITHE, FAKENHAM, 7 August 1912

This postcard shows a boat being rowed in the flooded roadway at Hall Staithe. The cottages, both on the left and on the right, have been demolished since this time, but the other building on the right, formerly a maltings, remains today.

HALL STAITHE, FAKENHAM, c.1924

Hall Staithe leads towards a narrow causeway path. This in turn leads to Hempton via a road bridge over the River Wensum. Here is the crossing point where Gogg's Mill was located, until 1934. Charlton's, a local brewery, stood in Hall Staithe until 1911, when it was demolished to make way for a sewage works and a fire station. The former maltings building remains in use today as commercial premises, but the cottages on the left have now disappeared.

TUNN STREET, FAKENHAM

Tunn Street, Fakenham's oldest street, leads out from the Market Square towards Mill Lane and Fakenham Mill. Those cottages on both sides of the street have been demolished. The site to the left is now used for the parking of cars. To the right is Havelock Square.

Fakenham Church, N.E.

ST. PETER AND ST. PAUL PARISH CHURCH, FAKENHAM, p.u. 1911

The church, which was probably built in the fourteenth century, stands beyond the northern side of the Market Place. In Arthur Mee's *Norfolk,* the houses and shops crowded around the church are likened to 'sheep to their shepherd'. The 115 foot-high tower may be ascended by 146 steps. Its clock face supports 'hands' that are 6 feet and 5 feet respectively in length. Extensive restoration took place in the Victorian era and again in recent years.

MARKET SQUARE, FAKENHAM.

THE MARKET SQUARE, FAKENHAM, c.1930

A horse-drawn wagon is seen next to the Market Square water pump. A signpost has replaced a gas lamp that was fixed to the top of the pump. Behind the shire horse the branch of the London City and Midland Bank has replaced former buildings on this site.

THE CROWN INN, FAKENHAM, c.1902

A former coaching inn, The Crown dates back some six hundred years. It stands, with rear stone courtyard, on the southern side of the Market Place, Fakenham. The inn advertises the Cyclists' Touring Club emblem on its front outer wall. To the extreme left of the picture is Bowles' milliners and outfitters shop; and G.W. Gosling, tailor and breeches-maker stands between this and the inn. To the right, the Drug Stores are advertised.

THE MARKET PLACE AND THE LION HOTEL, c.1905

In his diary of 1784, Parson Woodforde refers to dining at 'The Lion' and spending the afternoon in Fakenham. In this photograph a very high horse-drawn gig is driven past the Lion Hotel. This name was later changed to the Red Lion. The waterpump shown stood in the Market Place from 1870 to 1939. Above the large archway is the Cyclists' Touring Club emblem to mark the headquarters there at this time. Selling Bullard's ales and stout, the Lion also advertised that it had a bowling green, a billiard room and a 'lock-up house'. It closed as a hotel, in 1974, and now houses various council offices and the local tourist office.

(13) Market Place, Fakenham

MARKET DAY, FAKENHAM, c.1910

Fakenham has enjoyed the right to hold a market since 1250. An advertisement on the outer wall of the tailor's shop of Ecclestone and Son includes the statement 'we are absolutely the only firm who can employ a thoroughly up-to-date and expert cutter and will guarantee our customers a perfect fit.' Amid the market stalls activity, to the foreground, stands the town pump with gas-lamp holder and signpost. The latter has directions to both the M.&G.N. Fakenham West railway station and to the G.E.R. station.

MARKET DAY, FAKENHAM, p.u.1930

A busy Thursday market scene in 1930. The Midland Bank building, in the centre background, has replaced the former Ecclestone and Son shop premises. The bank on the right is Gurney's, which later became Barclays. The porch and windows of this building were later removed and a shop front fitted. Previously, Aldiss the outfitter occupied the premises which is now a shoe shop.

THE PROCLAMATION OF GEORGE V, 10 May, 1910

A splendid gathering of onlookers listening to the formal proclamation of the accession to the throne of His Majesty King George V, read aloud in the Market Square. Civic dignitaries are standing on the platform surrounded by members of the police force, the fire brigade, the military bands and many well-dressed members of public. Those at the open windows enjoy a 'grandstand' view.

NORFOLK YEOMANRY ON PARADE, 1914

On parade in the Market Square, Friday, 4 August, 1914, at the outbreak of World War I, is 'C' Squadron, the King's Own Royal Regiment, Norfolk Imperial Yeomanry. This regiment was first established in 1782 by Viscount Townshend of Raynham. The large Georgian house, in the background of the photograph, was the home and shop of the quaker, Edmond Peckover. He was a businessman and a merchant who later formed a partnership with Gurney's Bank, Fakenham.

PEACE CELEBRATIONS, 1918

A joyful crowd gathers in the Market Square to celebrate the end of the First World War. The partly demolished shop, to the right in the background, was replaced by the Midland Bank branch that stands there today.

UNVEILING THE WAR MEMORIAL, FAKENHAM, 1921

The unveiling ceremony at Fakenham's War Memorial is shown on this postcard. The town band is on the extreme right and the majority of gentlemen stand with their headwear removed. The photographer was R. Cable from Little Melton, near Norwich. The War Memorial replaced the memorial erected in 1902 to commemorate the coronation of Edward VII.

3123. THE WAR MEMORIAL, FAKENHAM.

THE WAR MEMORIAL, FAKENHAM, c.1925

This close-up view of Fakenham's War Memorial is shown on a postcard published by H. and H. Priest, Norwich Street. The Memorial was erected in 1921, in memory of those men of Fakenham who were members of the armed services and who gave their lives in the First World War. Those who gave their lives in the Second World War also had names added to the Memorial. Protective iron railings were later positioned around its base.

Stewardson & Co. Printers and Stationers, Fakenham

Meet of Harriers, Fakenham.

A MEET OF HARRIERS, FAKENHAM, p.u.1907

The Market Square was the venue for this meet of the harriers in Fakenham in 1907. The hunt has often met in the town, the most recent occasion was on Boxing Day, 1991. Clearly visible, in the left foreground, is the King Edward VII Coronation Memorial. Since this photograph was taken, the memorial has been moved to several different sites. Its present position is near the Oak Street library.

FIFE AND FORFAR YEOMANRY, CHURCH PARADE, FAKENHAM, 1915

The First Fife and Forfar Yeomanry on Church Parade at Fakenham, 20 June, 1915. These men camped on nearby Hempton Green, 18 April to 6 September, in that year. They formed part of the Highland Mounted Brigade, who were under the command of Brigadier General Lord Lovat, with their headquarters in Hunstanton. Other Highland Brigade regiments included the 1st and 2nd Lovat Scouts, the Field Ambulance RAMC, and the Inverness Royal Horse Artillery. Their camps were at Heacham, Harpley, Houghton and Little Massingham.

Fakenham.

The Wrench Series, No. 9456

Bridge Street.

BRIDGE STREET, FAKENHAM, p.u.1907

The view from the Market Place looking south down Bridge Street towards Fakenham's bridge and mill. On the right, E. Burbage, corn merchant, sold hay, straw, corn, flour and offal. Opposite is the Norfolk Café, and further down on the left, the Lancaster Commercial and Temperance Hotel and the Bull Inn. Whilst the latter is still in use today, all the premises on the right have been demolished.

NORWICH STREET, FAKENHAM, c.1935

On the right are the 'Chocolate Box' tea rooms where Mrs. E.D. Hastings was the proprietor. Next door was Chapman's, formerly Sayer's, the butcher's shop. Further down was Joseph Baker's hardware shop and Bone's Success Cycleworks. The popularity of motor cycle 'combinations' at the time is evident.

BIG FIRE AT FAKENHAM, 6 February, 1908

A multi-view postcard showing the effects of a fire at Joseph Baker's hardware shop, Norwich Street. The 'snapshots' were taken and published by an amateur photographer, T.J. Miller 'junior', who also owned the town's printing works. The intensity of the fire is evident in each picture.

NORWICH STREET, FAKENHAM, c.1908

This interesting social history postcard shows workmen, under the watchful eye of their bowler-hatted foreman, fitting a new front to the shop of F.W. Miller, bookseller, stationer and newsagent. Outside the premises, the handcart was used to convey builders' materials. In the left foreground, near the children, blankets are for sale.

NORWICH STREET, FAKENHAM, c.1946

An unusually deserted Norwich Street. The building on the left housed the offices of Fakenham's printing works. The building with the street light attached at its corner was formerly the Sun Inn. On the right is Jimmy Mews barber shop. This later became a shoe shop which has now closed.

Fakenham.

144705

THE POST OFFICE, QUEEN'S ROAD, FAKENHAM, c.1946

Standing at the junction of Holt and Queen's Roads is Fakenham Post Office. It was moved to this site from the Market Place in 1933. The Rampant Horse public house is to the left; the cottages on the same side, in the foreground, have since been demolished.

AFTERMATH OF THE QUEEN'S ROAD FIRE, FAKENHAM, 1913

This 'real photographic' postcard, published by May Bone of Fakenham, reveals the remnants of those buildings consumed by the fire on 3 August, 1913. These ruined premises, on the western side of Queen's Road, and opposite to what was a recently built secondary modern school, belonged to Mr. Needs. Fortunately, the 'new' school was not damaged by the fire.

STATION ROAD, FAKENHAM, p.u.1909

Station Road, also known as Norwich Road, leads away from the town to Fakenham's Great Eastern railway station. To the right is Baron's Hall Lawn, the home of the town's football and cricket clubs. The large house to the left is Belle Vue. This 'snapshot' was taken by H. Applegate, who had a photographic shop in Norwich Road itself. The message on this card includes, 'What do you think of this photo of Dorrie and Miss Henry?' It is assumed that Dorrie is in the distance pushing Miss Henry in the pram.

BARON'S HALL, FAKENHAM.

BARON'S HALL, FAKENHAM, p.u.1910

Baron's Hall, an elegant Georgian house built 1812, stands to the south of Station Road. The original hall and outer buildings, of which the barn is the only remnant, was purchased in 1593 by the Gwyn family for use as their home. During the Second World War, the Hall was used by local air-raid precautions personnel. The former Walsingham Rural District Council later used it as administrative offices. Today it has been converted into flats which overlook houses within its former grounds.

PRINTING WORKS FIRE, FAKENHAM, 21 November, 1914

A 'real photographic' postcard, by photographer May Bone of Fakenham, reveals the extent of the fire damage at T.J. Miller's printing works in White Horse Street. Only the chimney stack and wall ends are still standing amidst the charred remains of the premises. The factory was rebuilt and remained in use until its closure in 1982.

THE CATTLE MARKET, FAKENHAM, c.1904

Fakenham originally held its cattle market using temporary pens in the Market Place. Later it moved to Wells Road and, in 1857, to the permanent site shown between White Horse and Bridge Streets. This photograph shows a predominance of sheep in the market amidst a light fall of snow. The background cottages were demolished to make way for an extension to the Fakenham printing works. This in turn was eventually removed and is now a car parking area.

JUBILEE BRIDGE, RIVER WENSUM

The Jubilee Footbridge was built over the River Wensum to commemorate Queen Victoria's Golden Jubilee in 1887. A combined road and footbridge later replaced a ford crossing at this point. This postcard shows a happy group of children playing and paddling in the river, under the watchful gaze of an elderly rider on his sturdy horse.

FAKENHAM MILL, p.u.1941

This postcard shows Dewing and Kersley's flourmill which was down river from Gogg's Mill. Prior to 1833, when the bridge in view was built through public subscription, there was a ford at this point. The mill was owned by Joseph Fyson in 1854. It has since been converted into flats — with a restaurant in the building to the right — after the central brick chimney and the tall asbestos tower were removed.

FLOOD AT FAKENHAM MILL, 27 August, 1912

Local photographer May Bone produced this postcard view of Fakenham Mill as seen during the flood of 27 August, 1912. When a total of 7.5 inches of rain fell across the county of Norfolk widespread flooding occurred both in the city of Norwich and along the Wensum Valley. This card clearly shows the breached mill wall allowing the flood water to flow into the river. Later, a grating was included in the wall at this point to allow any future floodwater to flow through.

THE CAUSEWAY, FAKENHAM FLOOD, August 1912

This card shows floodwater from the swollen River Wensum and from the nearby meadows as it cascades over the causeway footpath onto the roadway. This causeway, lying on the route from Fakenham West station to Fakenham's mill, provides a source of enjoyment for the children seen paddling here.

THE CAUSEWAY, August 1912

Two horse-drawn vehicles venture along the flooded road leading from Hempton to Fakenham Mill. Some of the travellers have been named as Old Mick Dye, driving in the foreground cart, and in the rear, a Mr. Bassham drives Jack Powell. Mr. Bassham lived in Cygnet House in Swan Street.

The Causeway, Fakenham

THE CAUSEWAY, FAKENHAM, c.1913

This wide expanse of the River Wensum is shown on this view which looks eastwards to the rear of Fakenham Watermill.
The mill's tall brick chimney was a local landmark. On the right Fakenham's gas works, opened in 1846, can be seen.
These served the town until the 1960s. The premises now house a museum of gas and of local history.

FAKENHAM WEST RAILWAY STATION

On the west, or Hempton side, of the railway track stood a brick building. Goods' sheds, cattle-pens and yards completed the facilities on this side. A footbridge, also shown in the photograph, linked the west platform with the Fakenham side, where there was a small waiting room. The Lynn to Fakenham railway, served by this station, originated in a local Act of Parliament in 1876. The Midland and Great Northern Railway took over the former responsibilities from the Great Eastern Railway in 1893. The station finally closed 28 February, 1959, and with only part of its platform remaining, eventually became a builders' merchant's depot.

FAKENHAM EGG DEPOT, p.u.1904

Situated at Fakenham West railway station in Hempton is the Fakenham Poultry Society Egg Depot. A large goods wagon is visible to the right at the rear of the building. This postcard, sent to a local farmer in November 1904, offers him the equivalent of twelve and a half new pence for every twenty eggs he sends to the depot.

BAY HOUSE, SCULTHORPE, c.1935

Opposite to the Horse and Groom public house in The Street, Sculthorpe, stands Bay House and its bakery. This former home and baker's shop of the Tuck family is still in use today as a private residence.

The Street, Sculthorpe.

THE STREET, SCULTHORPE, c.1935

The village shop and post office are shown on the left of The Street, Sculthorpe. The Horse and Groom public house at the end of the street, offered Bullard's ales and stout and is still licensed today. Standing back from the roadway, on the right, stood the Greyhound, a former public house.

Grey's Mill, Sculthorpe.

GREY'S MILL, SCULTHORPE, c.1935

Grey's watermill, the first of its type on the River Wensum, stands about one mile to the south-west of Sculthorpe. Today, the mill has been converted into a hotel which includes the feature of a glass-plate section of floor through which one can see the river underneath.

BIBLIOGRAPHY

The information accompanying each postcard has been gleaned from a wide variety of sources: original documents, town and county directories, and published works — some of which are listed below.

Midland and Great Northern Railway Scenes	Clarke R.H., (1978)
A Guide to Castle Acre	Duckinfield Astley H.J., (1912)
The Boroughs Guide to Fakenham	Humphreys A.E., (1910)
Norfolk	Mees A., (1940)
A Popular Guide to Norfolk Churches	Mortlock D.P. and Roberts C.U., (1985)
The Building of Norfolk: North East Norfolk and Norwich	Pevsner N., (1962)
The Building of Norfolk: North West and South Norfolk	Pevsner N., (1962)
Long Ago in Swaffham	Smith G., (c.1900)

ACKNOWLEDGEMENTS

The author is indebted to the following people, without whom it would have been impossible to produce this book:

Philip Standley
My wife, June, for her help
Typing: Barbara Cockcroft
Editing: William Cockcroft, Brian Dolan, Steve Benz
Marketing: Steve Benz
Proof reading: Frank Rhodes

Local titles published by S.B. Publications in the series: "A Portrait in Old Picture Postcards"

The Soke of Peterborough
Peterborough, Then and Now
Peterborough, Vols. 1,2 & 3
Huntingdonshire, Vols. 1,2 & 3
Ted Mott's Cambridge
The Villages of Old Cambridgeshire

Hertfordshire, Vols. 1, 2 & 3

Southall and Norwood
Enfield
From Highgate to Hornsey
The Parish of St. Mary, Islington
Islington and Clerkenwell
Wandsworth

Eastbourne, Vols. 1 & 2
Seaford, Vol. 2
Brighton & Hove, Vol. 1
Pevensey and District

Norwich, Vols. 1, 2, 3 & 4
Holt and District
The Norfolk Broads
Thetford and District
Great Yarmouth, Vols. 1 & 2
West Norfolk
Diss and District
Sheringham and Beeston

Norfolk answers the call
Norfolk's Lifeboats
Norfolk's Railways, Vols. 1 & 2
Herring Heydays

Suffolk's Railways
Beccles and Bungay, Vols. 1 & 2
East Suffolk
Lowestoft, Vol. 1
West Suffolk

Other local titles available and in preparation. For full details write (enclosing S.A.E.) to:
S.B. Publications, c/o 19, Grove Road, Seaford, East Sussex, BN25 1TP.